30 Addition Puzzle

By

Julia Dunn

Introduction:

Have great fun solving the addition puzzle. This exercise book is specifically designed to sharpen the minds of little champs. It has 30 different addition puzzle exercises which will able the child to activate his brain.

EXERCISE # 1

	+		+		+		33
+		+		+		+	
	+		+		+		26
+		+		+		+	
	+		+	5	+		40
+		+		+		+	
16	+		+		+		37
32		38		25		41	

EXERCISE # 2

	+		+		+		47
+	■	+	■	+	■	+	
7	+		+		+		31
+	■	+	■	+	■	+	
	+	3	+		+		29
+	■	+	■	+	■	+	
	+		+		+		29
31		33		32		40	

EXERCISE # 3

	+		+		+		38
+	■	+	■	+	■	+	
	+		+		+		32
+	■	+	■	+	■	+	
1	+		+		+		30
+	■	+	■	+	■	+	
13	+		+		+		36
36		27		33		40	

EXERCISE # 4

	+		+		+		46
+		+		+		+	
1	+		+		+		13
+		+		+		+	
	+	3	+		+		38
+		+		+		+	
	+		+		+		39
43		21		44		28	

EXERCISE # 5

	+		+		+		24
+		+		+		+	
	+		+		+		37
+		+		+		+	
	+		+	8	+	3	33
+		+		+		+	
	+		+		+		42
30		54		37		15	

EXERCISE # 6

	+		+		+		24
+		+		+		+	
	+		+		+		37
+		+		+		+	
	+		+	8	+	3	33
+		+		+		+	
	+		+		+		42
30		54		37		15	

EXERCISE #7

13	+		+		+		42
+	■	+	■	+	■	+	
	+		+		+		34
+	■	+	■	+	■	+	
	+		+		+		34
+	■	+	■	+	■	+	
10	+		+		+		26
43		36		37		20	

EXERCISE # 8

	+		+		+			25
+	■	+	■	+	■	+		
	+		+		+			44
+	■	+	■	+	■	+		
	+		+		+	9		33
+	■	+	■	+	■	+		
	+	8	+		+			34
40		49		25		22		

EXERCISE # 9

	+		+		+		29
+		+		+		+	
	+		+		+		47
+		+		+		+	
	+		+		+		28
+		+		+		+	
	+	4	+	3	+		32
49		25		26		36	

EXERCISE # 10

	+		+		+		23
+		+		+		+	
	+		+		+		49
+		+		+		+	
	+	3	+		+		21
+		+		+		+	
	+		+	7	+		43
40		32		30		34	

XERCISE # 11

	+		+	7	+		21
+		+		+		+	
	+		+	1	+		23
+		+		+		+	
	+		+		+		45
+		+		+		+	
	+		+		+		47
30		45		23		38	

EXERCISE # 12

	+		+		+	13	35
+		+		+		+	
1	+		+		+		29
+		+		+		+	
	+		+		+		34
+		+		+		+	
	+		+		+		38
20		47		28		41	

EXERCISE#13

10	+		+		+		26
+		+		+		+	
	+		+		+		43
+		+		+		+	
7	+		+		+		22
+		+		+		+	
	+		+		+		45
36		36		33		31	

EXERCISE # 14

	+		+		+		42
+	■	+	■	+	■	+	
	+		+		+		35
+	■	+	■	+	■	+	
	+		+	6	+		21
+	■	+	■	+	■	+	
	+		+		+	2	38
19		38		48		31	

EXERCISE#15

	+	1	+		+		25
+		+		+		+	
	+		+		+		43
+		+		+		+	
	+		+		+		25
+		+		+		+	
	+	7	+		+		43
26		24		48		38	

EXERCISE # 16

	+		+		+		46
+	■	+	■	+	■	+	
	+		+	11	+	7	45
+	■	+	■	+	■	+	
	+		+		+		32
+	■	+	■	+	■	+	
	+		+		+		13
32		39		27		38	

EXERCISE # 17

	+		+		+	12	30
+	■	+	■	+	■	+	
	+		+		+		34
+	■	+	■	+	■	+	
	+	5	+		+		32
+	■	+	■	+	■	+	
	+		+		+		40
24		30		40		42	

EXERCISE # 18

	+		+		+		46
+	■	+	■	+	■	+	
7	+		+	10	+		27
+	■	+	■	+	■	+	
	+		+		+		13
+	■	+	■	+	■	+	
	+		+		+		50
38		31		41		26	

EXERCISE # 19

	+	10	+		+		35
+		+		+		+	
	+		+		+		22
+		+		+		+	
14	+		+		+		53
+		+		+		+	
	+		+		+		26
36		28		40		32	

EXERCISE # 20

	+		+		+		26
+	■	+	■	+	■	+	
	+		+		+		28
+	■	+	■	+	■	+	
	+	7	+		+		42
+	■	+	■	+	■	+	
2	+		+		+		40
33		40		30		33	

EXERCISE # 21

	+		+		+		31
+		+		+		+	
	+		+		+		29
+		+		+		+	
6	+		+		+		39
+		+		+		+	
5	+		+		+		37
19		39		49		29	

EXERCISE # 22

	+		+		+		28
+		+		+		+	
4	+		+		+		39
+		+		+		+	
	+		+		+	12	32
+		+		+		+	
	+		+		+		37
20		40		43		33	

EXERCISE # 23

	+		+		+		32
+	■	+	■	+	■	+	
	+		+	11	+		19
+	■	+	■	+	■	+	
	+	12	+		+		44
+	■	+	■	+	■	+	
	+		+		+		41
39		35		39		23	

EXERCISE # 24

1	+		+		+		24
+		+		+		+	
	+		+		+		47
+		+		+		+	
	+	2	+		+		35
+		+		+		+	
	+		+		+		30
26		39		37		34	

EXERCISE # 25

	+		+	8	+		23
+		+		+		+	
	+	15	+		+		45
+		+		+		+	
	+		+		+		41
+		+		+		+	
	+		+		+		27
37		35		30		34	

EXERCISE # 26

	+	10	+		+		24
+		+		+		+	
	+		+	6	+		32
+		+		+		+	
	+		+		+		42
+		+		+		+	
	+		+		+		38
33		36		27		40	

EXERCISE # 27

	+		+		+		34
+		+		+		+	
	+		+		+		49
+		+		+		+	
	+		+	4	+		28
+		+		+		+	
	+		+	5	+		25
52		22		32		30	

EXERCISE # 28

	+		+		+	7	40
+	■	+	■	+	■	+	
	+		+		+		36
+	■	+	■	+	■	+	
	+	16	+		+		42
+	■	+	■	+	■	+	
	+		+		+		18
32		42		31		31	

EXERCISE # 29

	+		+		+		28
+	■	+	■	+	■	+	
7	+		+		+		26
+	■	+	■	+	■	+	
	+		+		+		26
+	■	+	■	+	■	+	
	+	16	+		+		56
42		47		22		25	

EXERCISE # 30